God Is Love

God Is Love

William R. Lowery

RESOURCE *Publications* • Eugene, Oregon

GOD IS LOVE

Copyright © 2021 William R. Lowery. All rights reserved. Except for brief quotations in critical publications or reviews, no part of this book may be reproduced in any manner without prior written permission from the publisher. Write: Permissions, Wipf and Stock Publishers, 199 W. 8th Ave., Suite 3, Eugene, OR 97401.

Resource Publications
An Imprint of Wipf and Stock Publishers
199 W. 8th Ave., Suite 3
Eugene, OR 97401

www.wipfandstock.com

PAPERBACK ISBN: 978-1-7252-9320-5
HARDCOVER ISBN: 978-1-7252-9321-2
EBOOK ISBN: 978-1-7252-9322-9

02/18/21

Scripture quotations taken from the HOLY BIBLE, NEW INTERNATIONAL VERSON. ® *Copyright © 1973,1978, 1984 by International Bible Society. Used by permission of Zondervan Publishing House.*

Scripture quotations taken from the THE HOLY BIBLE, KING JAMES VERSION, Cleveland and New York, The World Publishing Company

I wish to give a special thanks to my wife Donna for her love, patience, and support without which, this would not have been possible.

Contents

Preface | ix

God is Love | 1
My God Called To Me | 3
How Could He | 4
Lord and Savior | 5
Great is My God | 7
My Responsibility | 9
Prince of Peace | 11
He's No Stranger to My Pain | 13
He is the God | 15
Now is the Time | 17
There in Bethlehem | 18
Praying | 20
Almighty God | 22
God's Gift | 25
Revelation | 26
Vivaldi's Rain (Of Love) | 28
Lord of All Time | 29
Your Only Hope | 30
The Path is Bright | 31
I'm Basking in the Love of God | 32
Angels in Three Parts | 34
Back Sliding Ways | 40

Reach Out and Embrace Him | 42
Jesus Christ | 44
His Love | 46
Christian | 48
He Is My God | 50
Great Is God's Love | 52
My Friend | 54
My House | 56
Timeless Treasures | 58
On A Cross | 60
Tear Stained Eyes | 62
My Prayer | 63
For All Time | 64
Oh Sin How Great Your Cost | 66
Love is the Gift God Gave to Me | 68
Holy Spirit | 69
In the Fullness of Time | 71
Lord Jesus | 73
While I Was Still Lost in Sin | 75
His Love's Complete | 77
From Saul to Paul | 79
How We Love Christ | 81
I Will Give Praise | 83
My Risen God | 85
My Savior | 87
God Gave His Son | 89
Will You Meet Me in Heaven | 94
The Love of Jesus | 96

Preface

I WANT TO GIVE all of the credit to God for these works. I am a retired chemical engineer without a poetic bone in my body and I would have never dreamed I would end up publishing a book of poetry.

This all started one Sunday afternoon with me on the couch minding my own business surfing the channels. I came across some lovely women in beautiful evening gowns singing wonderful music. I checked the channel and it was the local Public Broadcasting Station. It turns out that this was an annual PBS fund raiser featuring Celtic Woman for the first time.

I bought the CD and DVD of the concert and the next year when they returned for the annual fund raiser, I went to their live concert.

This could have been the end of the story, but one day I was listening to the Celtic Woman CD and my favorite song "Orinoco Flow" came on. It suddenly hit me that at one time music such as this would be dedicated to God. This is what should happen to this music. I then took this idea to friends with music/writing experience and got nowhere.

Discouraged, I realized if new words praising God were to be written, I would have to do it. To say this was a long shot is an under statement. Other than technical reports, I had not written anything since college English class.

When I listened to the music, something strange happened. The music started telling me the words. This is the case for all of the poems I have written. I listened to the music and the words came. I have had friends tell me they enjoy the poetry, but when I

Preface

read the works without music, I just see plain words. When I read them with the music, I am moved.

I hope these words are meaningful to you.

God is Love

We were lost, we were lost, we were dying in our sins
We were loved, we were loved, by our God Omnipotent
We have hope, we have hope, by his promised covenant
We'll be saved, we'll be saved, by his royal sacrifice

All hail, All hail, The loving Father
All hail, All hail, The Prince of Peace
All hail, All hail, The Holy Spirit
All hail, All hail, The Three in One
King of Kings, Holy, Merciful and Wise

God is love, God is love, God is love
God loves you, God loves me, God loves all
Jesus came, he obeyed, the Pure One
God is love, Three in one, he's our all

He was born, in a barn, to a virgin teenage bride
He was praised, he was told, by the angels in the sky
He grew up, he matured, in the town of Galilee
He left home, to preach love, to a lost and errant world

All hail, All hail, The loving Father
All hail, All hail, The Prince of Peace
All hail, All hail, The Holy Spirit
All hail, All hail, The Three in One
King of Kings, Holy, Merciful and Wise

> For God so loved the world, that he gave his only begotten Son, that whosoever believeth in him should not perish, but have everlasting life.
>
> For God sent not his Son into the world to condemn the world; but that the world through him might be saved.
>
> He that believeth on him is not condemned: but he that believeth not is condemned already, because he hath not believed in the name of the only begotten Son of God. John 3:16—18 KJV

God is love, God is love, God is love
God loves you, God loves me, God loves all
Jesus came, He obeyed, the Pure One
God is love, Three in one, He's our all

Poor were fed, sick were healed, God's Son shone upon the land
Prayer was taught, lame men walked, man forgiven of his sins
Church men balked, leaders talked, Satan's furry could be felt
There he hung, on a cross, a crown of thorns upon his head

He'll come back, he will reign, as the master of the world
He will rule, and he'll bless, God is Love, God is Love
He will judge, and he'll choose, His beloved from the lost
It's the end, no appeal, Mankind's fate forever set

He'll come back, he will reign, God is Love, God is Love
We are loved, we are loved, by our God Omnipotent
He'll come back, he will reign, God is Love, God is Love
We are saved, we are saved, by his royal sacrifice

He'll come back, He'll come back, God is love, God is love
He will reign, He will reign, God is love, God is love, God is love

God is love, God is love, God is love
God is love, Three in one, He's our all

Music/Praise Ministers:
This can be sung to the Celtic Woman version of "Orinoco Flow".

My God Called To Me

All alone in my sin, my God called to me
Lay your head in my lap safe, for eternity
I claimed his great love, all my sins washed away
You are mine now my dearest, saved this very day

I grew colder and proud, my own way I did go
Come home to me, little one, please, do not say no
I plotted my own life, it turned gray and cold
I love you, my dear child come, return to my fold

My life, in aimless sin, The Spirit stepped in
I do not cede my saved ones, My love will never end
So hungry for his love, to Jesus I plead
Welcome back, my loved one, your needs will be fed

Music/Praise Ministers:
This can be sung to the Celtic Woman version of "She Moved Through the Fair"

How Could He

How could he leave heaven above
And come down to earth
How could he live as a man
And suffer for my sins
He hung there all alone
Abandoned by his friends

His shed blood, his precious blood
Floods down and washes over me
Pure and good, and freely given
So gently wipes my sins away

How could he believe in me
Before I knew him
How could he still love me so
After my failings
His is God's only Son
His love there always for me

His shed blood, his precious blood
Floods down and washes over me
Pure and good, and freely given
So gently wipes my sins away
So gently wipes my sins away

Music/Praise Ministers:
This can be sung to the Celtic Woman version of "May It Be"

Lord and Savior

When I did meet my Lord and Savior
In the hour I first believed
What did he do but love and hold me
With his own life he made me clean
First he washed me, then he scrubbed me
With his dear hands and his own kiss
How could I ever expect
Such peace and joy and happiness

Oh for the love of my Lord Jesus
Oh for his loving grace today
Oh for the love of my Lord Jesus
Oh let me love him more each day

I grew to know my Lord and Savior
As my faith in him increased
What did he do but love and hold me
All my sins and debts erased
Now he takes my burdens from me
Carries them on his strong broad back
How could I ever suspect
That with such love I'll never lack

Oh for the love of my Lord Jesus
Oh for his loving grace today
Oh for the love of my Lord Jesus
Oh let me love him more each day

Truly I trust my Lord and Savior
He is faithful, good and just
What did he do but love and hold me
Filling my soul with happiness
Now my days are full of pleasure
Knowing my soul is safe and sound
How can I show my respect
For Jesus' love that does abound

Oh for the love of my Lord Jesus
Oh for his loving grace today
Oh for the love of my Lord Jesus
Oh let me love him more each day

Music/Praise Ministers:
This can be sung to the Celtic Woman version of "Spanish Lady"

Great is My God

Great is my God, and great is my love for him
Great is my God, and greater his love for me
Great is my God, He is so wonderful
He is my God and my brother and friend to me

When I walk with him, I'm never alone
I see his love shine, He'll always be there for me
For he is my strength, the light of my life
And how can I fail if only I follow him

Great is my God, and great is my love for him
Great is my God, and greater his love for me
Great is my God, He is so wonderful
He is my God and my brother and friend to me

The world beats me down, His love can be found
When grief comes to me, His comfort is all around
Depression takes hold, He lights up my soul
A better friend here, I never could hope to have

Great is my God, and great is my love for him
Great is my God, and greater his love for me
Great is my God, He is so wonderful
He is my God and my brother and friend to me

He came as a man, a ransom for sin
He died on a cross, to make my life whole and pure
He rose in three days, for all to behold
He reigns from above, His mercy pours down on me

He came as a man, a ransom for sin
He died on a cross, to make my life whole and pure
He rose in three days, for all to behold
He reigns from above, His mercy pours down on me

Great is my God, and great is my love for him
Great is my God, and greater his love for me
Great is my God, He is so wonderful
He is my God and my brother and friend to me

Great is my God, and great is my love for him
Great is my God, and greater his love for me
Great is my God, He is so wonderful
He is my God and my brother and friend to me

Music/Praise Ministers:
This can be sung to the Celtic Woman version of "Sí Do Mhaímeo Í"

My Responsibility

There are those poor lost souls who know not my God
They put their faith in their own mortal hands
But how can they find truth if I don't tell them
And they'll be lost for all eternity
His wondrous love they will not ever find it
And never know his joy and grace and peace
He told us all to go and spread his message
So it is my responsibility

But when I go and try to spread the gospel
Here in this cold and dark and doubting world
I lose my strength, my courage yes it fails me
And I shirk my responsibility

I dream of great and wondrous things I could do
I worship him, my tithe is freely giv'n
But I've refused to go and spread his good news
And wonder why so many are still lost
Now I must take his cross upon my shoulder
And to the fields of harvest I must go
No great deeds just tell a simple story
To fulfill my responsibility

But life is short
My hour on earth is ending
And soon the time will come to meet my God
When I face my Lord and Savior will he say
I fulfilled my responsibility

Music/Praise Ministers:
This can be sung to the Celtic Woman version of "Isle of Innisfree"

Prince of Peace

Dawning
And the beginning of a brand new day
Take me to Your bosom and hold me like a newborn babe

Sunlight
My beacon on a stormy way
Won't You be my guiding light for this another cold and dreary day

Trusting in the Prince of Peace
Knowing that his love's complete
What I'd really like to know
Is how he can love me so

Covered up in all my sins
Knowing I could never win
Nothing left to do
But put all my trust in You

Master, I know that You love me
I have no greater pleasure than Your spirit taking care of me
Savior, throughout my history
You have been my loving solace and kept my life from misery

Praying to the Prince of Peace
Knowing that his love's unique
What I'd really like to know
Is how he can love me so

Covered up in all my sins
Knowing I could never win
Nothing left to do
But put all my trust in You

Failings, there's plenty that I have
You reach right down and pull me up and wash me off white as snow
And pleasures, You've given me my share
I can live a life of joy secure that you are there to help me grow

Trusting in the Prince of Peace
Knowing that His love's complete
What I'd really like to know
Is how He can love me so

Praying to the Prince of Peace
Knowing that His love's unique
What I'd really like to know
Is how He can love me so

Covered up in all my sins
Knowing I could never win
Nothing left to do
But put all my trust in You

Trusting in the Prince of Peace
Praying to the Prince of Peace
Trusting in the Prince of Peace
Praying to the Prince of Peace

Music/Praise Ministers:
This can be sung to the Juice Newton song "Queen of Hearts"

He's No Stranger to My Pain

He's no stranger to my pain
He's my blessed savior
From my bad behavior, Christ protects me
I've fallen to my knees
Called out my desperate pleas
And he never gives up, his hand outstretched to me

He's no stranger to my pain
He forgives my failings
And he's quick to give me shelter in a crisis
He carries me in the bad times
Gives me hope and good signs
And all the time, I depend on him
He's no stranger to my pain

And when I turn away in weakness
When I'm feeling proud
Satan's there to help me fall right down
And it's hard to do the right thing
Ev'n when I know better
The sin and false pleasures hold me down
Now I really need him around

He's no stranger to my pain
And he's always there to cleanse me
He'll wrap his arms around me and he'll kiss me
And I'll come out of this stronger
With for his word a hunger
And to live a life that shows my love for him
He's no stranger to my pain

Oh, yes, He's no stranger to my pain

He's no stranger to my pain
He's my blessed savior
From my bad behavior, he protects me
And I'll come out of this stronger
With for his word a hunger
And to live a life that shows my love for him
He's no stranger to my pain

Oh, yes, He's no stranger to my pain

Music/Praise Ministers:
This can be sung to the Keith Whitley version of "I'm No Stranger to the Rain"

He is the God

He is the God of my life
And he has laid claim to my soul

Put down your pride and seek after Me
I am the God of eternity
I came to earth to set you free
Pick up your cross and come follow Me

He is the God, who created the universe
He is the God, of both heaven and earth
He is the God, and the Father of all our race
He is my God, He is supreme

He is the God, who chose Sarah and Abraham
He is the God, of the judges and kings
He is the God, who gave us the covenant
He is my God, for all men to know

He is the God, who promised deliverance
He is the God, to his word he is true
He is the God, who answers our prayers to him
He is my God, unto him honor is due

He is the God, who sent us his beloved Son
He is the God, through him vict'ry is won
He is the God, who hung on a cross for me
He is my God

He is the God, of the past who has always been
He is the God, of the present who is
He is the God, of the future
He is my God, He is my God
He is my God, He is my God

Music/Praise Ministers:
This can be sung to the Celtic Woman version of "The Voice"

Now is the Time

Now is the time, the time, to come and follow him
Oh don't you hear, his voice to you calls out
You can be sure, his love for you will never dim
Now you, yes you, must put away all doubt

Please turn to him, head bowed in soft humility
No payment you could make upon your own
And bask in his pure love offered without a fee
Oh poor lost child, please come and kneel down at his throne

And when you come, and your sins are all washed away
A boundless joy, you now will come to know
You'll find that sin no longer has you in its sway
But that his grace upon you now will flow

Now you hear his sweet soft voice gently guiding you
And all your life will now much sweeter be
Take comfort in that to His Word, he's always true
Once safely in his arms, his kind face you will see

Music/Praise Ministers:
This can be sung to "Danny Boy"

There in Bethlehem

There in Bethlehem
On a starlit night
Birth is taking place

A virgin bride awaits
The coming of her first born son
A simple peasant girl, a stable for a home

The time is coming due
With Angels watching over her
The Son of God is born, a child of lowly birth

Angels in the sky
Their voices praising God in song
The Heavens now proclaim
The coming of our King

Shepherds quake, at the sight
Of the Heavenly Host
Fear us not, we bring good news that's foretold

God's promise has been kept
The love of God came down as man
For unto you is born a Savior, Christ the Lord

Shepherds tell of his birth, to a waiting world
Wise men come bearing gifts for the newborn King

The Savior has been born
We celebrate his day of birth
On this first Christmas Day, God's love is now complete

Music/Praise Ministers:
This can be sung to the Celtic Woman version of "Walking in the Air"

Praying

Praying, Praying

This joy God's gift to me
No charge given for free
My Savior reigns in Heav'n above
And listens to me when I'm praying

Life's trials don't worry me
Laid before him to see
Knowing quite well he will be there
A comfort to me when I'm praying

Knelt down on bended knee
All sins confessed out loud
God's grace for me assured
His love for which I'm so proud

In joy to him I'll go
Jesus I love him so
My praises ring up to the sky
And near him I'll be when I'm praying

Praying

In time, this life will end I'll leave this shore
We'll meet apart no more
There in his arms you will find me
So safe and secure due to praying

Praying

Always praying
Always praying

Music/Praise Ministers:
This can be sung to the Celtic Woman version of "Beyond the Sea"

Almighty God

Lost in doubt and without hope
And did not have anyway to cope
I looked for strength and I found none
It seemed my life might end
All the wrong approaches I kept trying
They did no good they just left me crying
'Til one day I saw a light
It looked as bright as day

I was born in a Christian home
My name was put on a cradle roll
On mother's knee I learned his name
I've known him all my life
I worshiped him and in his word I grew
When I was eight I knew what I must do
To the world I did proclaim
That I was his that day

You are Christ the Great Redeemer
Who came down to earth from Heav'n above
Almighty God your love for me keeps me safe and strong
I know that you will always guide me
To be part of your Celestial Plan
Almighty God your grace rains down on sinful man

I plead for help and I keep on pleading
Please oh Lord give me what I'm needing
I am afraid you'll refuse my prayers
Because of how I've lived
Your love and grace freely given to me
Washing clean, pure, and sanctifying
I now am yours, your will no more defying
Saved from sinful ways

Now I've matured and I've kept on growing
And fought the fears that had me doubting
There were times when I kept on praying
I would not turn away
We have made it though those times together
With your help we will go on farther
Your love is with me you're the only reason
I am here today

You are Christ the Great Redeemer
Who came down to earth from Heav'n above
Almighty God your love for me keeps me safe and strong
I know that you will always guide me
To be part of your Celestial Plan
Almighty God your grace rains down on sinful man

I've kept the faith for many years
And with your help I confront my fears
My faith is strong and I do not worry
That you will go away
I sing your praises and it makes me proud
To worship you and say your name out loud
Now I have my place in Glory
Its waiting just for me

You are Christ the Great Redeemer
Who came down to earth from Heav'n above
Almighty God your love for me keeps me safe and strong
I know that you will always guide me
To be part of your Celestial Plan
Almighty God your grace rains down on sinful man

The evening comes the day is done
I've fought the fight and the race is won
My flesh is weak but my spirit's willing
To always keep the faith
My hour approaches and the time is nigh
Into your arms I will quickly fly
This earthly body I soon will lose
And then I will be home

You are Christ the Great Redeemer
Who came down to earth from Heav'n above
Almighty God your love for me keeps me safe and strong
I know that you will always guide me
To be part of your Celestial Plan
Almighty God your grace rains down on sinful man

Almighty God your grace rains down on sinful man
Almighty God your grace rains down on sinful man
Almighty God your grace rains down on sinful man

Music/Praise Ministers:
This can be sung to "Caledonia".

God's Gift

God's Son, God's great gift, his blood has set me free
He loved me so much, he died for me

He came, to save us, we nailed him to a cross
Hell's bonds were broken, he rose and he lives

He came from Heaven
He came from Heaven to save my soul

God's Son, God's great gift, his blood has set me free
He loved me so much, he died for me

He came to teach us, we did not listen
He bled for our sins, the perfect lamb
He rose victoriously and conquered death

He lives, in Heaven, he's waiting for the time
He will reign on earth, oh perfect of days

Music/Praise Ministers:
This can be sung to the Celtic Woman version of "Lascia Ch'io Pianga"

Revelation

He was the last, the friend of Christ
Prophesy told, just to him alone
The things to come, they now are known
Heed these words to John to whom was told

> Salvation belongs to our God
> Who sits on the throne, and to the Lamb
> Revelations 7:10 NIV

> Salvation belongs to our God
> Who sits on the throne, and to the Lamb
> Revelations 7:10 NIV

The seven churches, their fates are cast
Herald'd by the angels of the Lord
The seals are opened by the Lamb
And soon the earth will come to be no more

> Salvation belongs to our God
> Who sits on the throne, and to the Lamb
> Revelations 7:10 NIV

> Salvation belongs to our God
> Who sits on the throne, and to the Lamb
> Revelations 7:10 NIV

The time of darkness, it is to come
The seven plagues will torment man and beast
A horrible time, Oh woe to us
But the time of Satan, it soon will end

> Salvation belongs to our God
> Who sits on the throne, and to the Lamb
> Revelations 7:10 NIV

> Salvation belongs to our God
> Who sits on the throne, and to the Lamb
> Revelations 7:10 NIV

Then comes the time of the book of life
The old heaven and earth are there no more
The city of God, it shines with gold
It needs not light, it is the lamp of God

> Salvation belongs to our God
> Who sits on the throne, and to the Lamb
> Revelations 7:10 NIV

> Salvation belongs to our God
> Who sits on the throne, and to the Lamb
> Revelations 7:10 NIV

Music/Praise Ministers:
This can be sung to the Celtic Woman version of "Newgrange"

Vivaldi's Rain (Of Love)

You are my God and Savior
Who's love is never ending
You died for my sins so I could have eternal life
With my God in Heaven

I have no doubts my faith is strong
Your love will protect me
Nothing can take me away from You

There will come a time when I will be tempted
I am not afraid of the Dark One
I know that I will not be alone
Jesus' blood was shed so that I would not fear
I was lost and my sins would keep me from you

You will never forsake or turn from me
Mighty God please protect me from all evil
I give my life unto you Lord and Savior

Music/Praise Ministers:
This can be sung to Vivaldi's "Rain"

Lord of All Time

Did you know your sins caused our Lord's death
Tortured, scourged, rejected and shamed
He came to save us all from ourselves
His love is a gift from our God

As he hung there on that terrible cross
Tortured, scourged, rejected and shamed
Where were his friends who called him Lord
They were weak and he was so strong

My God my God why did You forsake me
Tortured, scourged, rejected and shamed
Put in a dark tomb and into Hell's hand
There he lay for me he did die

Death's chains were broken freed from the grave
Honored, loved, respected and praised
He rose to give us hope for our lives
Lamb of God the Lord of all time

Music/Praise Ministers:
This can be sung to "Scarborough Fair"

Your Only Hope

Your only hope is God's gift to you
Saved only by Christ's cleansing blood
No sin's too great for Jesus to save you
The foulest life only he can clean

But you said your life is beyond endurance
And you have no place to go
If you will put your faith in Lord Jesus
He'll carry your burdens and lighten your load

With God's great love I was sent redemption
A crown of thorns and an empty grave
His nail scarred hands hold me so softly
And my life now is his very own

Christ's gift is yours if you'll only ask him
Pardoned from sin all debts are paid
You will know his love and endless pleasures
Safely with him eternally

Come to him now while there is still time
Softly calling you to his side
No other option but to bow before him
Kneel before his cross and your sins lay down

Music/Praise Ministers:
This can be sung to "Carrickfergus"

The Path is Bright

The path is dark, I cannot walk it
I need a light, to guide me through
I've tried in vain, to make my own way
Hearth ache and pain, is all I found

O where can I find help and solace
The world's pleasures, have left me cold
My fortune buys, me only sorrows
An empty heart, is all I own

I heard a name, they call him Jesus
He loved me so, his life he gave
If only I, will call out to him
And ask his help, my soul he'll save

I knelt before, my Lord and Savior
And put my life, in his strong hands
He lifted me, from the cold and darkness
And led me back, to the light of day

The path is bright, when he walks with me
A guiding light, I've found in him
My life is full, since I found his joy
The Love of God, it lights my way

Music/Praise Ministers:
This can be sung to the Hayley Westenra version of "The Water is Wide"

I'm Basking in the Love of God

When Jesus told me that he loved me
My joy did not know any bound
For I knew that I did not deserve him
Or His blessed love which I just found
But my God will never leave me
Or ever lead me astray
So now I'm basking in the Glory of God

Oh yes I'm basking
In the glory of God
Ooh I'm basking in the glory of God
(Praise Father, Spirit, and Son
They rule Heaven as One)

When I follow the path he laid for me
I know the way will be straight and true
If I take my life and give it to him
There is nothing better I could do
For my God will always love me
And will lead me in his way
So now I'm basking in the glory of God

Oh yes I'm basking
In the glory of God
Ooh I'm basking in the glory of God

Yes my God will always love me
Even when I don't do right
So now I'm basking in the glory of God

Oh yes I'm basking
In the glory of God
Ooh I'm basking in the glory of God
(Praise the Father, Spirit and Son
They rule Heaven as One)

Music/Praise Ministers:
This can be sung to the Boyce & Heart version of "I Wonder What She's Doing Tonight"

Angels in Three Parts
Part I–The Birth

There's joy in the skies
The time is drawing nigh
God's Son will be born

The angels all draw near
They come to see if it is true
The Holy Son of God
Will live upon the earth

The messengers are picked
To deliver the blessed news
An honor guard is formed
To guard the virgin bride

First Mary must be told
The honor she has been bestowed
And Joseph put at ease
This is the Son of God

The journey is complete, Angels watching them
Time has come to go tell a waiting world

The shepherds will be told
The first to hear this glorious news
A chorus of the skies
To sing the newborn's birth

Legions are set in place to guard them from harm
The wise men are forewarned he is kept safe

The child grows wise and strong
The evils ones are kept at bay
The angels of the Lord
Keep watch from Heaven above

Music/Praise Ministers:
This can be sung to the Celtic Woman version of "Walking in the Air"

Part II–His Life

Angels are on guard
We watch over him
Keeping him from harm

Jesus is now a man
His ministry has now begun
We must stay vigilant he cannot come to harm

He's fasting in the wild
Now tempted by the evil one
He passes this first test, now to his side we fly

As he teaches men
We angels stand by on alert
Our fiery swords and shields are ready for his call

Angels gasp in disgust
How can this take place
Christ our Lord tried by men and sent to die

They're crucifying Christ
We cannot let this crime go on
We're ready to save him
Please give us the command

Angels rage, lightening strikes, the sky turns to black
The earth shakes, the veil is rent, the end has come

I'm sitting in a tomb
To tell the women he has gone
Now everyone can know
The glory of our Lord

Music/Praise Ministers:
This can be sung to the Celtic Woman version of "Walking in the Air"

Part III–His Kingdom

Now the time has come
Swords are being drawn
Battles will take place

The angels are a-stir
We're getting ready for the war
Our armor is aflame
Our swords are lightning sharp

A herald is chosen
To guide the servant of the Lord
The signs that he must see
And save for all to read

The seven seals are loosed
The trumpets of the Lord have blown
The plagues are on the earth
And man's fate is now known

Praising God with our voice for eternity
His power and glory for all to see

The beast is wild and free
His followers all bear his mark
They worship this false god
He leads them to to their death

Heavenly Host in battle gear fight the beast and win
Throwing him into the lake of fire and sin

We build a new city
It sits upon a hilltop high
God's city is with men
And he will live with them

Music/Praise Ministers:
This can be sung to the Celtic Woman version of "Walking in the Air"

Back Sliding Ways

I played the part and fooled the world no one knows what I think
Christ looked deep into my soul and saw that I would sink
I rule my life I thought this was just another day
Then he came to see me about my back sliding ways

I said I didn't need him, that time was long gone
His love to me he offered, why suffer all alone
I fought with him and argued I would do things my own way
Then he offered to help me change my back sliding ways

I come and go as I please, I answer to no man
I have my dreams of grandeur, I am my own best fan
But I felt deep down inside my heart the day would come to pay
And I would have to answer for my back sliding ways

I looked at him and questioned, what thing that I must do
He turned to me and took my hand and said his love is true
I fell right down before him and I began to pray
Oh please my Lord now help me shed my back sliding ways

My life has changed for better, as he told me it would
Now I run away from sin to live the life I should
So I pray to God and give him thanks for that glorious day
When Jesus came and freed me from my back sliding ways

Yes now I'm back with my Lord and praising his great name
For I am so thankful for the day he came
A sinner forgiven and so glad to say
That my Lord could save me from my back sliding ways

Music/Praise Ministers:
This can be sung to the Conway Twitty song "Tight Fittin' Jeans"

Reach Out and Embrace Him

Have you felt His compassion? Do you live in His love?
Is your heart open to Him? Are you saved from above?
He's been taking care of you, since before you were born
Jesus your Lord and Savior, all your sins he does mourn

If you'll turn your face to God, then your soul he will save
Christ's grand love will flow to you, the free gift that he gave
But your life will stay empty, without Christ in your heart
Now reach out and embrace him, from you he never will part

Saved by Christ, Life has meaning for the first time
I'm living in His Son-Shine, everything is so fine
I can feel his sweet love, this is such a good sign
Saved by Christ, Life has meaning for the first time

Are you ready for his love? Will you open your soul?
Will you make the commitment? And return to his fold?
Now's the time for an answer. Let your feelings show through
Now reach out and embrace him, and you'll see what he'll do
Now reach out and embrace him
Now reach out and embrace him
Now reach out and embrace him

Saved by Christ, Life has meaning for the first time
I'm living in His Son-Shine, everything is so fine
I can feel his sweet love, this is such a good sign
Saved by Christ, Life has meaning for the first time

Saved by Christ, Life has meaning for the first time
Saved by Christ, Life has meaning for the first time
Saved by Christ, Life has meaning for the first time
Saved by Christ, Life has meaning for the first time
Saved by Christ, My life has meaning for all time

Music/Praise Ministers:
This can be sung to the Head East song "Never Been Any Reason"

Jesus Christ

Where can I find redemption
From all my sins?, Jesus Christ

And who laid down his life for me
Given freely, Jesus Christ

God is so good, he is my friend, Christ loves me
His blood has washed my sins away
Unstained, reborn to him

What must I do to gain this
His love for me?, Jesus Christ

But all he asks is I follow
And I love him, Jesus Christ

God is so good, he is my friend, Christ loves me
His blood has washed my sins away
Unstained, reborn to him

I will kneel down before him
He's my master, Jesus Christ

And I will follow his teachings
Always reaching for his love
His joy fills my heart

Praise God in Heaven above
He rules with grace and love
The master of mankind
Glory to God King of all Kings

He fills me with his glory
He's my savior, Jesus Christ

And I have safety in his love
He protects me, Jesus Christ

My God, Jesus Christ
My God, Jesus Christ

Music/Praise Ministers:
This can be sung to the Enya song "Only Time"

His Love

First you were lost to sin, then came the Son
He washed your sins away, The Holy One
Christ paid the price for you, now you are free
His love is there for you, plainly to see

When you call out Christ's name, he will come to you
If you accept God's love, he will comfort you
When you follow his guide, he will love you too
If you open to Christ, your life will be new

You must accept God's love, call out his name
His face he'll turn to you, that's why Christ came
Then you'll feel his warm love, endless delight
Safe in his arms secure, all is now right

When you call out Christ's name, he will come to you
If you accept God's love, he will comfort you
When you follow his guide, he will love you too
If you open to Christ, your life will be new

You are now safe with Christ, others are lost
Who will tell them of him, and at what cost
If you are true to God, his word you'll spread
A dying world awaits, what must be said

When you call out Christ's name, he will come to you
If you accept God's love, he will comfort you
When you follow his guide, he will love you too
If you open to Christ, your life will be new

A life spent serving God, what a delight
Counting each day of love, there in His sight
A crown secure for you, Oh to behold
Your race is run and won, treasures untold

When you call out Christ's name, he will come to you
If you accept God's love, he will comfort you
When you follow his guide, he will love you too
If you open to Christ, your life will be new

Music/Praise Ministers:
This can be sung to the Enya song "Only If"

Christian

We are living in a world that is lost in sin
All are doomed if you don't try their souls to win
Christian oh why don't you share
With the ones who are lost to show that you care
Christian oh why don't you share
With the ones who are lost to show that you care
You were saved by Jesus' love and his Father's grace
You must go tell the world of his sweet embrace
Christian go seek out and tell
All the lost souls who're dying for to keep them from hell
Christian go seek out and tell
All the lost souls who're dying for to keep them from hell

Jesus gave us our command go and spread his word
How can we sit in silence and still call him Lord
Christian oh why don't you share
With the ones who are lost to show that you care
How can your heart be so hard
That you don't spread his message in your own backyard

Christ is sitting on his throne and he looks to us
For to go and spread his word and no doubt we must
Christian go seek out and tell
All the lost souls who're dying for to keep them from hell
Christian oh why don't you share
With the ones who are lost to show that you care
Christian oh why don't you share
With the ones who are lost to show that you care
How can your heart be so hard
That you don't spread his message in your own backyard

Music/Praise Ministers:
This can be sung to the Gordon Lightfoot song "Sundown"

He Is My God

He is my God, I will glorify his name
He is my God, From my mouth his praises ring
Jesus is my Lord and Savior
He is strong and my protector
I know all of my sins are washed away
He is my God, I will glorify his name

He is my God, his songs echo in the sky
He is my God, he reigns from his throne on high
His love is joy and compassion
I am saved by his resurrection
My soul is safe there is no doubt
He is my God, his songs echo in the sky

He is my God, I will glorify his name

He is my God, I will honor his commands
He is my God, I will go where he demands
And I will lay my life before him
As I see sin's pleasures grow dim
While I feel his power growing in me
He is my God, I will honor his commands

He is my God, I will glorify his name
He is my God, his songs echo in the sky
He is my God, I will honor his commands
He is my God, I will glorify his name

Music/Praise Ministers:
This can be sung to the Eric Clapton song "After Midnight"

Great Is God's Love

God in Heaven looked down on me
What hope did I have
Jesus spread his arms around me
I am safe with him

Great is God's love
It is endless
Always mine to claim
Oh what can this world offer to me when I have God's timeless love

As I walk the path before me
He is by my side
Daily trials, I don't fear them
He will lead my way

Great is God's love
It is endless
Always mine to claim
Oh what can this world offer to me when I have God's timeless love

When I stumble, he will catch me
Lest I should fall down
When storm clouds are gathered 'round me
His love will shine through

Great is God's love
It is endless
Always mine to claim
Oh what can this world offer to me when I have God's timeless love

At the end of this life's journey
And my time has come
Christ will welcome me in Heaven
There to live with him

Great is God's love
It is endless
Always mine to claim
Oh what can this world offer to me when I have God's timeless love

Music/Praise Ministers:
This can be sung to the Enya song "Long Long Journey"

My Friend

He is my God
I am his Servant
Bound to him
His word I will follow
All that I am
I owe to his love
Lost in sin
When he paid the price for me

I am his
I have no fear
My soul is safe now
Lovingly with him always
Unto Christ
I will honor
His name I will praise
Ever his love I will claim

I love him so
He is my beacon
A bright light
To guide and protect me
Ever a friend
There when I need him
Jesus Christ
My God and my savior Lord
I praise his name

Born to die and pay my debt
Sent by God spotless
Mocked by men then crucified
Raised from death to God's side

Born to die and pay my debt
Sent by God spotless
Mocked by men then crucified
Raised from death to God's side

Music/Praise Ministers:
This can be sung to the Enya song "The Celts"

My House

Lost ones, seeking meaning
In a world confused
There are so many choices
Where can they find Good News

Some say there is no God
They walk all alone
Their hearts are cold and empty
And all their hopes are gone

Some will turn to Buddha
They look deep within
While others pray to Allah
And hope they do not sin

Hindus worship all gods
Their souls never rest
And money is a cruel god
For it will take your best

Where can you find comfort
In a God who loves you
There is One who guides me
Jesus

Jesus always loves me
Even when I sin
His blood was shed to cleanse me
And wash me white again

Jesus is my Master
His name I will praise
No other god can claim me
They all fade into haze

As for me and my house
Yes we will serve the Lord. Joshua 24:15 KJV

As for me and my house
Yes we will serve the Lord. Joshua 24:15 KJV

Music/Praise Ministers:
This can be sung to the Enya song "Pilgrim"

Timeless Treasures

Sitting in the Darkness
Waiting sunrise
Listening to the sounds
Of the forest waking
Peaceful and contented
One with nature
Only God can make this day

Looking at a mountain
From a valley
As the Autumn leaves
Bathe the slopes with hues
Colors all around me
Reds and yellows
God's beauty glows this day

Catching snowflakes
On our noses
Oh the joy
Of a children's game
Winter like a blanket
The ground covers
Beauty shines when skies are gray

Lying by a river
Water flowing
Gently as it goes
Down a rocky pathway
Sometimes quickly
Others slowly
This is how God made the day
Beautiful are all God's days

Hiking in the forest
In the springtime
Watching as the squirrels
Leap and play above me
All around is new life
Young and tender
All can see God's love shine
On a peaceful valley
Full of sunlight
Flowers in the field
Make the ground blaze brightly
Looking at God's glory
Timeless treasures
Freely given to me
As I look to heaven
And the sun sets
There the clouds turn red
And dew starts falling
Far above the stars blink
Shine and twinkle
Knowing that God made this day
This is how I see his way
In the beauty of his day
Only God could make this day

Music/Praise Ministers:
This can be sung to the Enya song "Flora's Secret"

On A Cross

God is Great—God is Love—God is Kind—God is Joy
God is Pure—God is Wise—God is Strong—God is Good

God loves me
From my sins I am free
He wept then he cried for those who tortured him
And he paid my fee
I now sit at his knee
He wept and he died for those who tortured him for me
.
On a cross he did die
With his blood my sins were cleansed

How can he
Have so much love for me
He wept then he cried for those who tortured him
And his love's the key
For his death on that tree
He wept and he died for those who tortured him for me

From the grave he did rise
By his grace my soul is saved

God as Three
All my needs he can see
He wept then he cried for those who tortured him
My God cares for me
And my needs he does feed
He wept and he died for those who tortured him for me
He wept and he died for those who tortured him for me

I will be
His so all men can see
He wept then he cried for those who tortured him
And his grace is free
To a world lost in need
He wept then he died for those who tortured him for me
He wept then he died for those who tortured him for me
He wept then he died for those who tortured him for me

Music/Praise Ministers:
This can be sung to the Enya song "One By One"

Tear Stained Eyes

His tear stained eyes gazed down on me
As he hung nailed to a rough hewn tree
Twisted in pain Christ called my name
As he gave his love to claim

I held God's gift and made it mine
In my heart I'll keep it for all time
My life I've laid in his strong hands
Subject to my King's commands

My God so loved me
That he gave his own Son
An atonement for my sins
Paid with his own guiltless blood

God's joy is free for all to share
Jesus bled and died to prove he cares
If you will seek his will to know
He will wash you white as snow

Music/Praise Ministers:
This can be sung to the Enya song "A Day Without Rain"

My Prayer

Lord before Your throne I kneel down
For with Your love my life has been blessed
Delve deep into my soul, Oh God
Where my hidden sins are confessed

Holy Spirit hear my plea
Intercede now for me, with God

By Your hand my needs are met
And with Your truth You guide my way
Oh Lord I seek to gain Your grace
And the strength for this day

Holy is the Lord God
Holy is the Lord God
Holy is the Lord God, Amen

Mighty is the Lord God
Majestic is the Lord God
Holy is the Lord God, Amen

Music/Praise Ministers:
This can be sung to the Enya song "Deora Ar Mo Chroí"

For All Time

Your love for me is for all time
And that's the source of my peace of mind
First You saved me then, You took me in
And freed me from the chains of my sin
There was nothing else I could do
But bend my knee and bow down to You
Life was hopeless with nowhere else to go
You love me so
This I know
Your love is so great for me
In my soul what do You see
I can feel Your love in my life

Your love for me is all that I need
My faith I'll show by both word and deed
I will honor love and praise Your name
From my mouth Your love I'll proclaim
I'll bow down to You
And always seek Your word which is true
Love will save me, I will ever make it mine
My soul is Thine
I feel fine
Your word will always be my light
Lord lead me in the way that's right
I know Your love lives in my life

When my life is through
That's when I will come to see You
You redeemed me, with Your blood I was bathed
For I am saved
My debts waived
You will be there to take me home
My soul will never have to roam
I will share Your love for all time

Music/Praise Ministers:
This can be sung to the Fleetwood Mac song "Monday Morning"

Oh Sin How Great Your Cost

God made the world in his image
A garden he did share
All were at peace with God on earth
Man lived without a care

But then one day we chose to sin
And paradise was lost
Expelled to face a cold hard world
Oh sin how great your cost

Cut off from God a hope appeared
A man God chose to bless
For Abram was a righteous man
Who set out on God's quest

From Abraham there rose a hope
A savior born to man
Christ gave his life to pay my debt
The only one who can

Washed in his blood I took his name
As Savior and as King
His words I'll spread his will obey
His praises I will sing

Christ will return and claim his Throne
His glory ever bright
And sin will die a fiery death
In God's city of light

Music/Praise Ministers:
This can be sung to the Enya song "How Can I Keep From Singing" or "Amazing Grace"

Love is the Gift God Gave to Me

This world's cares weigh me down
But I know what to do
There is One I can trust
A friend to help me through
Jesus is always there
He takes me by the hand
Christ will lead me straight and true
Far from sinking sand

Love is the gift God gave to me
Love is the gift God gave to me

When I let Christ lead me
I don't have to fear
He can sail through stormy seas
A pathway always clear
His word's true this I know
It leads me every day
So I seek to know his will
And follow in his way

Love is the gift God gave to me
Love is the gift God gave to me

Music/Praise Ministers:
This can be sung to the Beatles song
"You've Got to Hide Your Love Away"

Holy Spirit

You have stood up for me from the day I was born
Never left me alone unloved or forlorn
I plead to You and You hear my prayer
You take my words and re-make them so God will hear
And Your love for me is clear
Jesus Christ lives as my Lord and my King
Of his grace all the angels do sing (praise his name)

Holy Spirit You are my friend
Comfort it pours out upon me
Holy Spirit my heart You do mend
A view of God I can see it
God in three persons does lead
Filling all of my needs
Oh Lord how is it You love me so
Holy Spirit please help me grow
My Lord please don't ever let me go

I have strayed from Your word and I know that hurts You
Turned my back on Your love oh the things that I do
And when I fall and can't get up
You come to me and I know I will be alright
Saved from an awful fright
Jesus Christ lives as my Lord and my King
Of his grace all the angels do sing (praise His name)

Holy Spirit You are my friend
Comfort it pours out upon me
Holy Spirit my heart You do mend
A view of God I can see it
God in three persons does lead
Filling all of my needs
Oh Lord how is it You love me so
Holy Spirit always stay with me
You're strong and I am so weak
Holy Spirit Your love's there to see
Your word is my goal to seek

Holy Spirit You are my friend
Comfort it pours out upon me
Holy Spirit my heart You do mend
A view of God I can see it
God in three persons does lead
Filling all of my needs
Oh Lord how is it You love me so
Holy Spirit please help me to grow
My Lord please don't ever let me go

Music/Praise Ministers:
This can be sung to the ABBA song "Mamma Mia"

In the Fullness of Time

I was deep in sin
When my heart You could win
You appeared to me
And Your love I could see
They told me how You came
And sacrificed Your life as payment
There upon a cross
In the fullness of time

I was full of life
But in my heart was strife
I followed my own way
And yet my world seemed gray
But still You cared for me
And offered me Your full redemption
There upon a cross
In the fullness of time

The angels sing Your praise
The glory of Your resurrection
I can hear the sound
As it echoes down from Heaven
Such a lovely sound
Because You always cared
Your loving hand was there
Free for me to take
A decision I must make

To follow in Your steps
And claim the grace You conquered death with
There upon a cross
In the fullness of time

The angels sing Your praise
The glory of Your resurrection
Angels sing Your praise
Angels sing Your praise
The glory of Your resurrection
Up until that day
Up until that day
I could do things my way
Then I had to stand
And saw You at God's right hand
You looked at me and cried
Away from me I never knew you
There at judgment day
I was lost for all time
I was lost for all time
I was lost for all time

Music/Praise Ministers:
This can be sung to the Moody Blues song "Your Wildest Dreams"

Lord Jesus

Jesus came as man
So he could feel my pain
He was crucified
Just for my redemption
Jesus is my Savior
I am his forevermore

I am always loved
He is always with me
I can feel his grace
As his love flows through me
Jesus is my Savior
I am his forevermore

I will praise, I will praise my Savior
I will praise, I will praise Jesus Christ
I will praise, I will praise my Savior, Lord Jesus

He is always there
And will ever guide me
I will never fail
When his will I follow
Jesus is my Savior
I am his forevermore

Every day is his
I will do his bidding
Shining in his light
I will sing his praises
Jesus is my Savior
I am his forevermore

I will praise, I will praise my Savior
I will praise, I will praise Jesus Christ
I will praise, I will praise my Savior, Lord Jesus

I will praise, I will praise my Savior
I will praise, I will praise Jesus Christ
I will praise, I will praise my Savior, Lord Jesus

For God sent not His son into the world
To condemn the world but that the world
Through Him might be saved John 3:17KJV

I will praise, I will praise my Savior
I will praise, I will praise Jesus Christ
I will praise, I will praise my Savior
I will praise, I will praise my Savior
I will praise, I will praise Jesus Christ
I will praise, I will praise my Savior,Lord Jesus
I will praise, I will praise my Savior, Lord Jesus

Music/Praise Ministers:
This can be sung to the Enya song "Wild Child"

While I Was Still Lost in Sin

While I was still lost in sin
Christ came as my Savior
I rejected him back then
For the world I loved more

Then his sweet voice called my name
A sound of kindness
Christ has taken all of my blame
So I could be sinless

Saved by grace through Christ my King
Now I have his pardon
From my mouth his praise I'll sing
His love I'll rely on

I asked him into my heart
Now he reigns as Lord
Joined as one we'll never part
I'm following his word

A new life I am living
His comfort I do feel
His grace to me he's giving
And his love is so real

Saved by grace through Christ my King
Now I have his pardon
From my mouth his praise I'll sing
His love I'll rely on

While I was still lost in sin
Christ came as my Savior
He called and my heart he did win
I'll love him forever

He called and my heart he did win
I'll love him forever

Music/Praise Ministers:
This can be sung to the Tim Harden song "If I were a Carpenter"

His Love's Complete

God sent His Son, he loves me so
Christ lives for me, this I do know
I can feel his presence, in my life today
He is there to guide me, on my stormy way
I am loved by Jesus
Every hair is counted by his hand
I am loved by Jesus
In his grace I know I'll always stand
His love's complete, it's all I need

I strive to serve, and do his will
To live apart, his law fulfill
I will spread his Gospel into every land
Working for my Savior, every way I can
I am loved by Jesus
Every hair is counted by his hand
I am loved by Jesus
In his grace I know I'll always stand
His love's complete, it's all I need
His love's complete, it's all I need

When my time ends, and I lie down
He'll come to me, with a gold crown
And I'll see the glory of my God on high
Safely in his arms now, nevermore to die
I am loved by Jesus
Every hair is counted by his hand
I am loved by Jesus
In his grace I know I'll always stand
His love's complete, it's all I need
His love's complete, it's all I need

Music/Praise Ministers:
This can be sung to the ABBA song "I Have A Dream"

From Saul to Paul

In Nazareth there lived a man
Who came from Heaven to complete God's plan
He taught of God's love so that all could hear
Then he bore our sins so we need not fear

The time had come men were spreading his word
A man named Saul disliked what he heard
When Stephen was stoned Saul held their coats
He chased Christ's saints, Oh to hear him gloat

John, Peter, Mathew, Philip, Thomas and James
Disciples of Christ all priests in his name
Saints of the Lord all born of the Son
Were spreading God's word oh the souls they won

Saul was full of pride as he hunted saints down
On the Damascus road Jesus Christ he found
A blinding light followed by God's voice
Christ said to Saul, I'm here to give you a choice

John, Peter, Mathew, Philip, Thomas and James
Disciples of Christ all priests in his name
Saints of the Lord all born of the Son
Were spreading God's word oh the souls they won

Saul heard God's words and he knew he had sinned
Ananias came and Saul's soul he did win
Saul became Paul and God's word he did preach
Paul sold out for Christ, so lives he could reach

That man now called Paul became a saint
When preaching Christ's name, he never was faint
Paul followed God's word, he lived in Christ's grace
He fought the good fight, he finished the race

John, Peter, Mathew, Philip, Thomas and James
Disciples of Christ all priests in his name
Saints of the Lord all born of the Son
Were spreading God's word oh the souls they won

John, Peter, Mathew, Philip, Thomas and James
Disciples of Christ all priests in his name (fade)

Music/Praise Ministers:
This can be sung to the Royal Guardsman's song "Snoopy Vs. the Red Baron"

How We Love Christ

Music is the way we will praise our God
With our voices, we will sing
To the heavens, we will praise
That's the way, we will show, how we love Christ

Prayer is the way we will praise our God
In the stillness, of our hearts
Calm and humble, we will praise
That's the way, we will show, how we love Christ

Service is the way we will praise our God
In our labors, we will work
With our own hands, we will praise
That's the way, we will show, how we love Christ

Sharing is the way we will praise our God
With our talents, every way
Freely given, we will praise
That's the way, we will show, how we love Christ

Teaching is the way we will praise our God
To our children, to the world
Spreading his word, we will praise
That's the way, we will show, how we love Christ

Study is the way we will praise our God
From the Bible, we will learn
Reading scripture, we will praise
That's the way, we will show, how we love Christ

Meeting is the way we will praise our God
In his temple, every day
Bowed before him, we will praise
That's the way, we will show, how we love Christ

Music/Praise Ministers:
This can be sung to the Donovan song "Colours"

I Will Give Praise

Praise, I will give praise
To my God
With my voice
At all times

Love, I'll show his love
By my speech
And my deeds
In my life

I was lost in a life of sin
Tried to cope but I could not win
Saw his light shine from above
Took Christ's hand, he saved me with his love

Peace, I have his peace
Christ's my God
I am safe
In his arms

Joy, I have his joy
My hearth sings
Of his grace
Unto me

My God lived and died for me
Crucified there at Calvary
But his life it did not end
He arose and now he is my friend

Christ's my savior, And protector, He is ever true
Jesus loves me, Always leads me, I bow down to him

My faith is on solid ground
I was saved when Christ's love I found
His angels watch out for me
Washed of all sin my soul is free

Saved, by God's love

Music/Praise Ministers:
This can be sung to the Moody Blues song "Ride My See-Saw"

My Risen God

My Lord will come again
And the vict'ry win
Christ will rule with love
When he comes from Heaven above

My Lord lives and Christ's reign will last forever
He will break the chains
Of the sins that bind us
And I'll praise, praise, praise
My risen God, my living God

My Lord lives and Christ's reign will last forever
He will break the chains
Of the sins that bind us
And I'll praise, praise, praise
My risen God, my living God

Christ's light will shine like gold
Just as the Bible told
His glory will soon fill
God's city on the hill

My Lord lives and Christ's reign will last forever
He will break the chains
Of the sins that bind us
And I'll praise, praise, praise
My risen God, my living God

My Lord lives and Christ's reign will last forever
He will break the chains
Of the sins that bind us
And I'll praise, praise, praise
My risen God, my living God

And I'll praise, praise, praise
My risen God, my living God (fade)

Music/Praise Ministers:
This can be sung to the June Carter Cash song "Ring of Fire"

My Savior

I will worship my Savior
Now and for all time
Yes, now and for all time
His blood washed me, Glory
His life saved me, Oh yes
My soul is redeemed

I will honor my Savior
At his throne I'll bow
Yes, at his throne I'll bow
His blood washed me, Glory
His life saved me, Oh yes
My soul is redeemed

I will follow my Savior
Where he leads I'll go
Yes, where he leads I'll go
His blood washed me, Glory
His life saved me, Oh yes
My soul is redeemed

Jesus can be your Savior
If you'll just ask him
To come into your heart
His blood will wash you, Glory
His life will save you, Oh yes
Your soul will be redeemed

We will worship our Savior
Now and for all time
Yes, now and for all time
His blood washed us, Glory
His life saved us, Oh yes
Our souls are redeemed

Music/Praise Ministers:
This can be sung to the We Five song "You Were On My Mind"

God Gave His Son
Solo

When I saw the wonders that my God had made
They made me feel oh so small
How did I fit in God's celestial plan
Was there a place for me at all

Overwhelmed with guilt and without one plea
I did not know what to do
Then I heard of a savior who died for me
They said his love is always true

God gave his Son to pay for my sins
His love for me, he showed it knows no bounds
Washed by his blood
So at judgment day, I need not make a sound
Guiltless as a babe
I kneel down to him

What do I do
They said I had to ask him
To come and live within my heart

He reached out
Took my head and laid it in his lap
And then he washed me
Clean so my new life could start

Praise the Lord, his love reached out to me
He pulled me out of my sinking sand

Glory fell from above
I can live my life today
Wrapped in Christ's unending love

God gave his Son to pay for my sins
His love for me, he showed it knows no bounds
Washed by his blood
So at judgment day, I need not make a sound
Guiltless as a babe
I kneel down to him

Living in God's family, I am still in awe
Of all the things he has done
But I need not worry about my lot in life
Because the vict'ry has been won

There are those who tell you that I gave life up
That faithful day
When I bowed down and asked Christ to be my King

Then my old life did end
But a new life began
And Christ's glory I will proudly sing

(God gave his Son)
Washed by His blood (to pay for my sins)
Saved from my sin (his love for me)
Praise his name
(God gave his Son)
(So at judgment day)
I will praise his name (I need not make a sound)
My God (God gave his Son)
I will praise.-.I will honor.-.I will serve him

(God gave his Son)
Just for me
He gave his life (his love for me)
(It knows no bounds)
(God gave his Son)
My God
I will praise his name (So at judgment day)
(I need not make a sound)
(God gave his Son)
I bow down to him

Music/Praise Ministers:
This can be sung to the Prince song "Raspberry Beret"

Hymn

When I saw the wonders that my God had made
They made me feel oh so small
How did I fit in God's celestial plan
Was there a place for me at all

God gave his Son to pay for my sins
His love for me, he showed it knows no bounds
Washed by his blood
So at judgment day, I need not make a sound
Guiltless as a babe
I kneel down to him

Overwhelmed with guilt and without one plea
I did not know what to do
Then I heard of a savior who died for me
They said his love is always true

God gave his Son to pay for my sins
His love for me, he showed it knows no bounds
Washed by his blood
So at judgment day, I need not make a sound
Guiltless as a babe
I kneel down to him

I begged for his mercy which he gave to me
It fell as rain from above
Basking in his glory, I could feel his grace
Wrapped in Christ's unending love

God gave his Son to pay for my sins
His love for me, he showed it knows no bounds
Washed by his blood
So at judgment day, I need not make a sound
Guiltless as a babe
I kneel down to him

Living in God's family, I am still in awe
Of all the things he has done
But I need not worry about my lot in life
Because the vict'ry has been won

God gave his Son to pay for my sins
His love for me, he showed it knows no bounds
Washed by his blood
So at judgment day, I need not make a sound
Guiltless as a babe
I kneel down to him

Music/Praise Ministers:
This can be sung to the Prince song "Raspberry Beret"

Will You Meet Me in Heaven

Oh our Savior's blood for us is cleansing
This he gave, This he gave
His grace to us he is bestowing
He will save, he will save

Will you meet me in Heaven reborn into light
In a new body there for all time
We'll live to praise our Savior
In the glory of our God
That is the thing I pray for all the time

There's a choice you must make to be made whole
Claim his love, Claim his love
Then his grace will flow down into your soul
Like a dove, Like a dove

Will you meet me in Heaven reborn into light
In a new body there for all time
We'll live to praise our Savior
In the glory of our God
That is the thing I pray for all the time

You will find your life has new meaning
Praise his name, Praise his name
And your soul will be constantly singing
Of his fame, Of his fame

Will you meet me in Heaven reborn into light
In a new body there for all time
We'll live to praise our Savior
In the glory of our God
That is the thing I pray for all the time

Will you meet me in Heaven reborn into light
In a new body there for all time
We'll live to praise our Savior
In the glory of our God
That is the thing I pray for all the time
That is the thing I pray for all the time

Music/Praise Ministers:
This can be sung to the Porter Wagoner and Dolly Parton song "Last Thing On My Mind"

The Love of Jesus

I was living the life that I thought I wanted
I did everything my own way

But somehow I saw that my life was empty
All I did was live for today

It was a Sunday morning when I heard the church bells
A feeling welled up in my soul, I had
Never felt that way

I went into that church and heard about Jesus
And the emptiness within me
Suddenly went away

Jesus is the one who heals all my heartaches
He will carry my load, when my soul is weary
Always here to comfort me, his love never failing
I am held safely in his grace
Striving to know his face
Of one thing I am sure
That his love is real, So real.

When I felt the love of Jesus in my life
Things I once loved seemed so far away
The empty heart I once had is full now
Overflowing with God's manna, I am blessed for another day

I will work for my Lord and tell of his story
And from my mouth I will sing praises, praises to his name

I have God's word to study and to learn from
The power of God to shield me, protection I can claim

Jesus is the one who heals all my heartaches
He will carry my load, when my soul is weary
Always here to comfort me, his love never failing
I am held safely in his grace
Striving to know his face
Of one thing I am sure
That his love is real, That his love is real

Now I've tried and I've failed and been forgiven
He's always there to guide me, his love rains from above
I know I have a place in Heaven
Until that day I will work to tell the world of your love
The love of Jesus
The love of Jesus

Music/Praise Ministers:
This can be sung to the Crosby Nash and Young song "Southern Cross"

www.ingramcontent.com/pod-product-compliance
Lightning Source LLC
LaVergne TN
LVHW051659080426
835511LV00017B/2636